Writings on the Wall

Writings on the Wall

Inspirational Poems & Quotes

Robert M. Hensel

Copyright © 2016 Robert M. Hensel

All rights reserved. No part of this book may be reproduced or transmitted in any form or by any means, electronic or mechanical, including photocopying, recording, or by any information storage and retrieval system, except in the case of brief quotations embodied in critical articles and reviews, without prior written permission of the publisher.

The author has made every effort to ensure the accuracy of the information within this book was correct at time of publication. The author does not assume and hereby disclaims any liability to any party for any loss, damage, or disruption caused by errors or omissions, whether such errors or omissions result from accident, negligence, or any other cause. The information contained within this book is strictly for educational purposes. If you wish to apply ideas contained in this book, you are taking full responsibility for your actions.

Printed in the United States of America

To my parents, Linda H. Conzone, and Robert J. Hensel, for all their love and support, throughout the years.

Table of Contents

Peace of Mind	1
America's Symbol	3
Nights Reflect	5
Peaceful Ground	7
Nature's Katrina	9
Natures Dance	11
Message of Love	13
End Racism	15
Poetry at Play	17
Jazzy Soul	19
A Small Town Disaster	21
Beyond Limitations	24
A Window of Pain	26
Expansion of Love	28
Poetic Warfare	30
Inside of Thee	32
Winter's Offerings	34
Dreams of Travel	36

Let it Be	38
The Need To Change	40
Fears of Night	42
Sheltered By The Truth	44
The Promise of A Rainbow	46
Body, Heart, and Soul	48
Pass The Torch	50
The Greatest Love	52
Winter's Gig	54
The Passing of Time	56
Where Hearts Run Free	58
A Lesson to Learn	60
Land of Independence	62
Throw My Heart Away	64
One Race	66
Straight Vessel	68
Price of a Heart	70
Interlink to Peace	72
If I Didn't Have You	74
Price of Freedom	76
Where Broken Hearts Lie	78
The Poet	80

Peace of Mind

Carry me out to the ocean, where my

drifting thoughts flow free.

Guide them to a far distant land, that

only the mind can see.

There I shall paint a great portrait, of what

this world should be.

A place without senseless wars, and

human poverty.

Food for Thought

I'm chasing my dreams straight to the top,

into a sky that has no limits.

—Robert M. Hensel

America's Symbol

It was through broad stripes and bright stars, that

this great Nation has been born.

A symbol of our freedom, that has continued to be worn.

America, united we stand, proud of our long beliefs.

That all who wish to live among it's land,

shall forever share in it's peace.

Food for Thought

We are the true architects of our lives. Only we as individuals and individuals alone, carry within us, the inner ability to make any changes to it's blue prints.

—Robert M. Hensel

Nights Reflect

Shadow puppets on the wall.

Dark carbon copies, of what

a furnished room bares.

Into a black covered mirror,

my world reflects.

Showing me things, only the

night has to offer.

Food for Thought

Whenever we begin to feel as if we can no longer go on, hope whispers in our ear, to remind us "We are strong."

—Robert M. Hensel

Peaceful Ground

Cool morning spit on bladed grass.

A thousand silky fingers tickling toes.

The strong scent of natures freshly cut hair.

Mans spiritual stomping ground, toward inner peace.

Food for Thought

Inspiration comes from the places we suffer the most.

—Robert M. Hensel

Natures Katrina

The ocean wages war against coastal land.
It's intentions quite clear, destroy modern man.
With it's powerful artillery eagerly drawn, the enemy storms on and on.
Pounding it's victims with enormous force.
Through wind and rain, it remains it's course.
Breaking down levies and tearing down trees.
Transforming whole cities, into stagnant seas.
Much life has been lost, by one tragic event.
The brutal attack, natures katrina has sent.

Food for Thought

Tears are the body's raindrops of emotion.

—Robert M. Hensel

Nature's Dance

I sit ashore this moonlit beach.
Where water, and sand, come
to meet.
As waves crash against the sandy
ground, together they will dance to
nature's sound.
One step, two steps, onto the shore.
Then comes back to dance some more.
This rhythmic view, I've come to glance.
The life that's found in nature's dance.

Food for Thought

Have courage enough to accept what you can not change, but yet, courageous enough to stand up and fight for what you can.

—Robert M. Hensel

Message of Love

Unveil onto me, the true message of
the heart.
Fill me with it's knowledge, so I may
learn the art.
Supply me with the needed tools, to
create a lasting love.
One, not even cupid and his arrows,
has ever heard of.

Food for Thought

No one has ever died, from an overexposure to education.

—Robert M. Hensel

End Racism

We all must bring our racism to an end.

A message to all, I long to send.

The colors of the world, all join as one.

For the lord is our shepherd, and we as his son.

Christ made all man in the likes of him.

So please, let us all end racism.

Food for Thought

A positive attitude, can turn a storm into a sprinkle.

—Robert M. Hensel

Poetry at Play

A poem is but a thought, a mere
memory caught at play.
One's visions reenacted, by the
passing of each day.
Treasured waking moments I've
accumulated along the way,
shall be locked within these pages,
where they're forever bound to stay.

Food for Thought

Feel the presence of love, wrapped up within a hug.

—Robert M. Hensel

Jazzy Soul

Playing the sax with chipmunk cheeks, boy man,

that brass really blows.

Slap me with those screaming beats, that fills

a jazz mans soul.

Food for Thought

It only takes but one seed of peace, to create a forest.

—Robert M. Hensel

A Small Town Disaster

It happened one summers afternoon.

In a small suburban town, off highway

eighty two.

I watched with amazement, as it dropped

out from the sky.

This giant enormous cloud, that had turned

category five.

Twisting and turning, as it moved across the

land.

Crushing helpless precious life, beneath it's

powerful raging hand.

No remorse for the victims, that lied tight within

it's grip.

It continued leveling the town, into a lifeless

graveyard pit.

Where homes once stood, only rubbish remains.

In a small community, caught in the middle, of

natures violent rage.

Food for Thought

There is no greater disability in society,

than the inability to see a person as more.

—Robert M. Hensel

Beyond Limitations

Placing one foot in front of the other, I've climbed

to higher Lengths.

Reaching beyond my own limitations, to show

my inner strength.

No obstacle too hard, for this warrior to overcome.

I'm just a man on a mission, to prove my disability

hasn't won.

Food for Thought

A man is not wealthy, simply by the contents of his pockets alone, but instead, by the richness of his heart.

—Robert M. Hensel

A Window of Pain

I look beyond a window of pain.

A fragment of glass, with tears that stain.

My life of sorrow, brings out a fire.

To write of things, that to me, inspire.

My thoughts are put into a poem.

Giving my words, a voice of their own.

Printed on paper, is the pain that I leave.

Releasing myself, of all that I grieve.

Food for Thought

I have never encountered a problem,

that optimism couldn't solve.

—Robert M, Hensel

Expansion of Love

Build your world around me, and promise to never let me go, and if ever comes a time it may seem crowded, may we expand so love may grow.

Food for Thought

Let your courage and determination be the vehicle that drives you, and takes you anywhere in this life you wanna go.

—Robert M. Hensel

Poetic Warfare

A pen to a poet, becomes a
mighty sword.
When drawn, a literary war against
paper, creatively unfolds.

Food for Thought

Man has been searching for the true meaning of life since the very beginning of time, and still, we have just scratched the surface. As we as humans evolve over time, maybe one day that answer will be found, but until then, may we continue to share what we have learned and discovered, during our time here, so that the next generation may have a stable foundation to build upon.

—Robert M. Hensel

Inside of Thee

I kneel down before the shallow waters,

to reveal my own reflection.

Just a mere window of the soul, is all

that my eye's can be detecting.

For what all that I consume, is not all

that there is.

We must look beneath the visual shell,

for that is where we live.

Reach deep my friend, and you shall find,

much more than conceive.

For who, or what, we may become, exists

inside of thee.

Food for Thought

It doesn't matter which side of the tracks your from,

the train still rolls the same.

—Robert M. Hensel

Winter's Offerings

Crispy chimes of autumn, spread out

upon natures floor.

The falling greens of Spring and Summer,

now taking on a brown like decor.

Bare bodies stand naked, their bones clanging

in the wind.

Hoping to soon be re-clothed, by winters cool

new offerings.

Food for Thought

Success is measured simply by the amount of effort we put forth, in conquering our objectives.

—Robert M. Hensel

Dreams of Travel

As I sit beneath a shaded tree.

I dream of exotic places, I'd

like to be.

From Spain on a mid Summer's

afternoon.

To sipping on elegant wines, one

night in Cancun.

One minute New York, next Seattle.

These are my dreams.

My dreams of travel.

Food for Thought

When the heart speaks, love listens.

—Robert M. Hensel

Let it Be

Let it be, that I may someday,

touch the stars.

When all time for me has expired,

and the soul begins to part.

Guide me through the heaven's

where life one day began.

A perfect creation, molded right out

of our Father's loving hands.

Food for Thought

To find equality for mankind, we must first remove the barriers that have divided us for so long.

—Robert M. Hensel

The Need to Change

Here is a message, that just can't be ignored.
The environmental hazards, that our planet has endured.
Through clouds of smoke, we suffocate it's air.
Not seeing it's true danger, so why should we all care.
The poisoning of it's waters, brought by human defect.
As we pound the ozone layer, with the very same neglect.
The future of it's existence, we hold into our hands.
Shall it be disposed of, such answer, lies with man.

Food for Thought

We are grains of sand resting along the shore.

Waiting to be washed away, till there is no more.

—Robert M. Hensel

Fears of Night

Darkness surrounds this room
that live.
Shadows cast figures, that blackness
shall give.
Transforming a room of unknown
sight.
To bring onto to me, my fears of
night.
Unrealistic thoughts of open gates.
A Wall of vision my mind creates.
Through my eye's these things are
real.
My fears of night, that I still feel.

Food for Thought

Compassion is one of the greatest forms of human expression. Learn the art!

—Robert M. Hensel

Sheltered by the Truth

A heart can't conceive what the mind
comprehends.
The essence of ones love, brought
down to bitter ends.
Letting go of entities that the minds
already been shown.
Loves last and final ending, that
the heart still fights to hold.
Not willing to distinguish, of what the
characters portraying.
A heart full of lies, that the minds
contemplating.
We look through a glass, with just
one side.
Sheltered by the truth, that lurks us
from inside.

Food for Thought

❦

It takes an open minded individual to look beyond a disability, and see, that ability has so much more to offer, than the limitations society tries to place upon them.

—Robert M. Hensel

❦

The Promise of a Rainbow

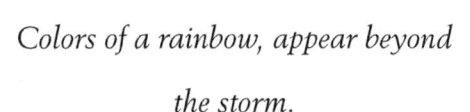

Colors of a rainbow, appear beyond

the storm.

Gods promise to all Nations, that through

flood no earth be torn.

Behind every darkened cloud, that builds in

heavens sky, will be his unforgotten words,

tomorrow shall never die.

Food for Thought

Dare to walk the path that others have feared to travel, and a leader shall then be born.

—Robert M. Hensel

Body, Heart, and Soul

If the body were a tree trunk, the inner rings would surely begin to reveal the time it has had to mature.

If the heart was an open book, it would then be placed on the New York Times best sellers list, as one of today's best romantic novels ever written.

If the mind was a time capsule, it would then be capable of holding onto every one of life's precious moments, without ever having the chance of fading away.

Food for Thought

A brush of kindness, can paint a smile on a face.

—Robert M. Hensel

Pass the Torch

This is my plea to all Nation's, Please lay down
all your weapons and guns.
Come sit at our table, lets talk, so the wars
they may be done.
Let the vehicle of democracy be our driven
force.
To serve as an example to your neighbors,
and dare to pass the torch.
Let it's bright light be your guide, and it's flame,
what warms your heart.
Tell me, isn't that how world peace really begins,
and allies seem to start?

Food for Thought

Time is our only true enemy. Slowly, it robs us of the one precious thing we can not bottle.

—Robert M. Hensel

The Greatest Love

My heart holds you tender, within it's

loving arms.

Always and forever, to shelter you

from harm.

Together, as a team, we shall build our

walls around.

The greatest love known to man, that you

and I have found.

Food for Thought

A fighter is someone who rises up,

even when the odds are stacked against them.

—Robert M. Hensel

Winter's Gig

Howling winds of winters song, blows

it's trumpet, all night long.

In comes a choir all dressed in white,

to join in the magic of cool delights.

Together, they form in its celebration.

A seasonal gig, of collaboration.

Food for Thought

When everyone else says you can't,

determination says, "YES YOU CAN."

—Robert M. Hensel

The Passing of Time

Hands of time move us forward,

never back.

Only memories frozen in mind,

can we reenact.

Food for Thought

Limitations are nothing more than optical illusions, created by our own self-doubt.

—Robert M. Hensel

Where Hearts Run Free

I know of a place, where hearts

run free.

High across the valley, open

sea.

Together we sail, as if were one.

Down beneath the surface, this

love shall run.

Into a current of lasting flow.

A place that all our hearts must

go.

Across the desert, into the sea,

this is the place, where hearts

run free.

Food for Thought

Sometimes it takes us traveling outside our comfort zone, to discover the abilities, we never knew we had.

—Robert M. Hensel

A Lesson to Learn

Everyday I fight to break down

these walls.

To reach beyond what judgements,

man has installed.

Behind concrete dividers, my crippled

body waits.

For the day society will come to learn,

from all it's mistakes.

Food for Thought

Life isn't all about what you don't have, but yet, what you do with what you have been given

—Robert M. Hensel

Land of Independence

I listen to the sound of freedom's bells
ring.
Chiming to a peaceful song, our fore
Father's sing.
American the beautiful, I'm free to walk
your land.
No restrictions put upon me, for the
person that I am.
This gift of independence, shall forever
stand tall.
Just look up at the American flag, it's
shinning for us all.

Food for Thought

Every failure is just another step closer to a win.

Never stop trying!

—Robert M. Hensel

Throw my Heart Away

Why did you have to go, and throw my
heart away, when my love, I gave so much of,
each and every day.
Are the dreams we had, lost forever.
All those special times we shared together.
Don't you know, I've cried so many tears
for you.
So how can you just walk away, and say that
we are through.
Like some kind of stranger in the night, I watch
as you walk out the door.
For I guess you don't really love me, anymore.
There is no words to say, when you throw
my heart away.

Food for Thought

Never take more out of life,

than you intend to give back.

—Robert M. Hensel

One Race

I cannot, and will not judge, by what

my eye's may see.

For the skin on a man, shall not reveal

his true identity.

Food for Thought

Face life head on...It's a collision you can't ignore.

—Robert M. Hensel

Straight as a Vessel

*There may be troubled waters
along the many paths my life
shall take, but only I as a man,
may keep my vessel afloat, and
guide myself straight.*

Food for Thought

❧

Life is a temporary position. When our jobs done,

we turn out the lights and go home.

—Robert M. Hensel

❧

Price of the Heart

No scale to balance whats in my heart.

No numbers to measure, nor even to

chart.

This love can't be seen in ounces, or

in pounds.

For only through time, can it's value

be found.

Food for Thought

No disability or dictionary out there, is capable of clearly defining who we are as a person. It's only when we step out of that labeled box, that our abilities begin to be fully recognized, giving us a better definition of who we truly are as individuals.

—Robert M. Hensel

Interlink to Peace

May the words that flow between the lines,

connect us to a world of peace.

Food for Thought

We all have a purpose in life,

no matter how big or small the role.

—Robert M. Hensel

If I Didn't Have You

If I didn't have you, could the

sun ever shine.

Would my eye's be able to hold

you, in this empty place of time.

If I didn't have you, would all good

things come to end.

Could my heart stand up to torture,

that your words may come to send.

Would each tear that falls from heaven,

come down to me as rain.

To rise up every answer, that fills my

heart with pain.

I pray these words I've spoken, shall

never they come true.

For my heart could not survive, if I

didn't have you.

Food for Thought

In order for us to reach success,

we must first find the ladder.

—Robert M. Hensel

Price of Freedom

Peace doesn't exist within the
barrel of a gun.
Only democracy can untangle,
what mankind has done.
Our flag, it has been stained, by the
very blood our soldiers lost.
I ask you Mr. President, how much does
Americas freedom, really cost?

Food for Thought

Knowledge must start with someone or something, whether it be self knowledge or taught to us by others.

—Robert M. Hensel

Where Broken Hearts Lie

Careless whispers, from out of the dark.
Not a vision, but a voice, crying deep within my heart.
The sound of it's pounding, travels far across a room.
As it searches for an exit, from the pain that's made it through.
Tell me, where do all the broken hearts lie?
Underneath a river of tears, ever lonely hearts cried.

Food for Thought

Find your passion in life, and make love to it.

—Robert M. Hensel

The Poet

Words flow onto paper like rain, forming
giant rivers of unseen lands.
The very force guides us along a journey,
that holds of great adventure.
We are the explorers of the literary world.
We must find the courage to write what others
are unable to, with the greatest of passion.
A poet dreams, and then must portray his visions,
upon the page that lies before him.
It is the beauty of all things, that inspires us to
communicate in such a way.
A man does not wake up one day, and decide
to become a poet.

It must live in the very blood that courses through his veins.

He is the creator of a world, only he has known.

He is the actor and director, of all that speaks out through his pen.

He is a man of all men....visionary of all visionaries.

What you haven't seen, he has.

What you can't say, he can.

For he is, the poet.

Food for Thought

We chip away at the impossible, in hopes of carving out the possibility of success.

—Robert M. Hensel

Printed in Great Britain
by Amazon